S0-EHY-413
3 4028 08214 6888
HARRIS COUNTY PUBLIC LIBRARY

April Fool's Day Jokes to Tickle Your Funny Bone

Enslow Elementary
an imprint of

Enslow Publishers, Inc.
40 Industrial Road
Box 398
Berkeley Heights, NJ 07922
USA
http://www.enslow.com

Special thanks to Sandy Beck, education director, The Wild Classroom, St. Francis Wildlife Rehabilitation Center, Tallahassee, Florida.

Enslow Elementary, an imprint of Enslow Publishers, Inc.

Enslow Elementary® is a registered trademark of Enslow Publishers, Inc.

Library of Congress Cataloging-in-Publication Data

LaRoche, Amelia.
April Fool's Day jokes to tickle your funny bone / Amelia LaRoche.
p. cm. — (Funnier bone jokes)
Includes index.
Summary: "Read jokes, limericks, tongue twisters, and knock-knock jokes about April Fool's Day. Also find out fun facts about the holiday"—Provided by publisher.
ISBN 978-0-7660-4122-6
1. Wit and humor, Juvenile. 2. April Fools' Day—Juvenile literature. I. Title.
PN6166.L37 2013
818'.60208—dc23
2012007697

Future editions:
Paperback ISBN 978-1-4644-0180-0
ePUB ISBN 978-1-4645-1093-9
PDF ISBN 978-1-4646-1093-6

Printed in the United States of America

092012 Lake Book Manufacturing, Inc., Melrose Park, IL

10 9 8 7 6 5 4 3 2 1

To Our Readers: We have done our best to make sure all Internet Addresses in this book were active and appropriate when we went to press. However, the author and the publisher have no control over and assume no liability for the material available on those Internet sites or on other Web sites they may link to. Any comments or suggestions can be sent by e-mail to comments@enslow.com or to the address on the back cover.

Every effort has been made to locate all copyright holders of material used in this book. If any errors or omissions have occurred, corrections will be made in future editions of this book.

♻ Enslow Publishers, Inc., is committed to printing our books on recycled paper. The paper in every book contains 10% to 30% post-consumer waste (PCW). The cover board on the outside of each book contains 100% PCW. Our goal is to do our part to help young people and the environment too!

Illustration Credits: Clipart.com, pp. 3, 5 (top), 7 (top), 9, 10 (top, middle), 12 (bottom), 13, 16, 18, 19 (top), 22 (bottom), 24, 25 (bottom), 26 (middle), 27 (bottom), 28 (top), 29, 31 (top, bottom), 32 (bottom), 33, 34, 35 (top), 36, 37 (top), 38 (bottom), 39, 41 (top, middle), 42 (top, bottom), 43; Photos.com: Adolfo Medina Licon, p. 37 (middle), Alexey Bannykh, p. 23 (bottom), Allison Bair, p. 19 (bottom), Anderson & Anderson, p. 10 (bottom), anna filitova, p. 7 (top), Bob Ash, pp. 22 (top), 32 (top), 35 (bottom), Cruz Puga, p. 15 (bottom), Dean Such, p. 25 (top), dedMazay, p. 11 (top), Dynamic Graphics, pp. 1, 4, 5 (bottom), 37 (bottom), Ganna Didora, p. 42 (middle), joaquin croxatto, p. 8 (middle), Lesia Biloshytska, p. 20 (bottom), Natalia Bannykh, p. 44 (top), Oleksander Kovalenko, p. 21 (top); Shutterstock.com, pp. 6, 8 (top, bottom), 11 (bottom), 12 (top), 14, 15 (top), 17, 20 (top), 21 (bottom), 23 (top), 26 (top, bottom), 27 (top), 28 (bottom), 30, 31 (middle), 38 (top), 40, 41 (bottom), 44 (bottom), 45.

Cover Illustration: Shutterstock.com

Contents

1 A Fool Is Born

Knock, knock!

Who's there?

Alex.

Alex who?

Alex the questions around here!

How many fools does it take to change a lightbulb?

One hundred: one to hold the lightbulb and ninety-nine to spin the house around.

Why couldn't the fool play cards on the boat?

He was sitting on the deck.

Why was the fool wet?

His shirt said, "Wash and wear."

Limerick

Before playing a masterful prank
First ask yourself this—and be frank:
Does it hurt anyone?
Or is it good fun?
Will the tricked person laugh and say, "Thanks"?

DID YOU KNOW?

Did you know that hundreds of years ago, many royal courts in Europe had a fool? It's true! Fools wore goofy costumes, told funny jokes, and did silly dances. These court jesters were allowed to make fun of the king and queen, but they had to be careful about how far they went. Fools who were too sassy sometimes got punished. The word *fool* comes from the Latin word *follis,* which basically means "windbag."

Why did the fool tiptoe past the medicine cabinet?

He didn't want to wake the sleeping pills.

April showers bring fools flowers.

Why did the fool throw his alarm clock out the window?

He wanted to see time fly!

How did the fool find the flea bite on her body?

She started from scratch.

Knock, knock!

Who's there?

Cash.

Cash who?

Bless you!

Jokes and pranks have been around for a long, long time. You have to wonder: Did one caveman tell the other caveman that his bone buttons were undone, and then flick him in the nose when he looked down to check?

Only fools duel with fuel!

Fooling Around the World

Knock, knock.

Who's there?

Jamaica.

Jamaica who?

Jamaica lot of international calls? My phone bill is huge!

Limerick

When you're sent to find something great,
Like striped paint, hen's teeth, a long weight—
Wherever you are,
Before looking too far,
You'd best ask yourself: "What's the date?"

FUN FACT

Did you know that people all over the world get in on the fun of April 1? It's true! People in China, Iraq, Turkey, the United States, and just about everywhere else enjoy playing pranks and having a good laugh on April Fool's Day. In some countries—like England—it's bad luck to play a trick after noon. Anyone who does is likely to be teased with a chant that goes something like this: "April Fool's Day is past and done, and you're the fool for making one!"

The map doesn't slate silliness for one spot.

What type of umbrella does the King of Sweden carry on a rainy day?

A wet one.

What did the fool say when the tourist asked him about the rain in his part of the world?

"It's little drops of water falling from the sky."

WHAT IS A LIMERICK?

Limericks are poems with five lines. Lines 1, 2, and 5 have seven to ten syllables and rhyme with one another. Lines 3 and 4 have five to seven syllables and also rhyme. When you read them out loud, you can hear the beat. They are usually funny, quite often they're "punny," and when they end with a twist, they're complete!

Why did the elephant miss his train to Liberia?

He forgot his trunk.

The world unfurls its fools' flags every April first.

Knock, knock!

Who's there?

Irish.

Irish who?

Irish you'd let me in. It's cold out here!

Why do people in Iceland do their laundry in Tide?

Because it's too cold out Tide.

Why did the fool fly around the world?
It was too far to walk.
Where did the fool go to find a wife?
Mississippi.
Why did the fool travel all the way to Australia?
He heard parakeets were going cheep there.
What do you call a gigantic ape in China?
Hong Kong.

3 Why Televisions Are Called "Idiot Boxes"

Hey, man, why did the ship's captain go to the news station?

Because he needed an anchor, man.

Swiss spaghetti strands stand straight up.

What was the name of the lion tamer who made the evening news?

Claude.

What do ducks like to watch?

Duckumentaries.

What did the rooster say about his favorite show?

"That's hen-tertainment!"

What did the weatherman at the North Pole say when his wife asked for the forecast?

"I predict rain, dear."

DID YOU KNOW?

Did you know that a very respected TV news show in England called *Panorama* tricked its viewers on April Fool's Day in 1957? It's true! A serious-sounding announcer said Swiss farmers would have a huge crop of spaghetti that spring. Footage showed peasants plucking strands of spaghetti from trees. Many viewers called the show to ask how they could grow a spaghetti tree! (The station told them to put a piece of spaghetti in some tomato sauce and then hope for the best.) The viewers must have, um, *forgotten* that spaghetti is made from flour and water, not grown on farms.

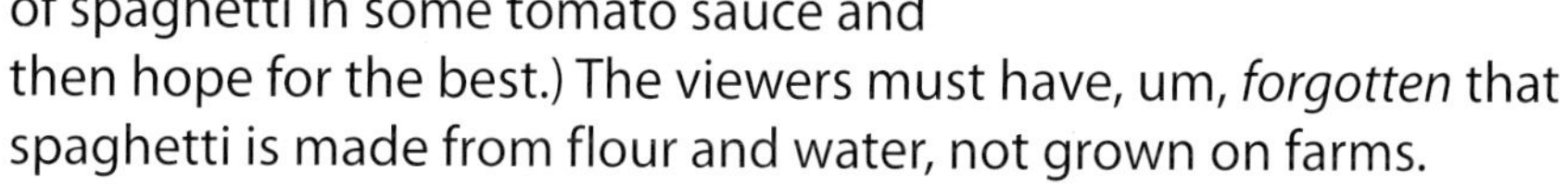

FUN FACT

In 1962, Sweden's only TV channel said that thanks to new technology, viewers could convert their black-and-white sets to color. The station's technical expert said all they had to do was pull a nylon stocking over their television screen. Then he showed them how to do it. Supposedly thousands of people tried it Color broadcasts didn't begin in Sweden until four years later.

WHAT IS A RIDDLE?

Riddles are questions with surprise answers. The goofier the answer, the funnier the riddle! Sometimes, a riddle makes you think, like this one: I am the beginning of the end, and the end of time and space. What am I? The letter "e"!

What did the foolish weatherman say?

"Today will be bright and sunny with a 90 percent chance that I'm wrong."

What did the fool do after he saw a news story about a man wanted for robbery?

He went to the TV stati
and applied for the jo

Did you hear they discovered a new blind dinosaur?

Scientists are calling it the I-don't-think-it-saurus.

What did the caterpillar say to her friend as they watched the program about butterflies?

"You'll never get me up in one of those things!"

Knock, knock!

Who's there?

Alison.

Alison who?

Alison if you tell me a joke.

Smell-O-Vision sends strange scents.

Knock, knock!

Who's there?

TV.

TV who?

TV or not TV? That is the question.

What do you get when you cross a sports reporter with a potato?

A common tater.

4 You've Been e-Pranked! Pranks on the Internet

Why did the fool refuse to log on to the World Wide Web?

He was afraid of spiders.

Why did Adam offer Eve a PC?

He didn't want her to pick the Apple.

Knock, knock!

Who's there?

Penny.

Penny who?

Penny for your thoughts.

DID YOU KNOW?

›id you know that the Internet needs
ɔ be shut down for cleaning once a
ear? It's true! Well, actually, it's *not* true.
ut many people got an e-mail in 1997
varning them that the Internet would
e closed on April 1 for "spring cleaning."
eople who got the e-mail were told to
urn off their computers that day so that
nternet-crawling robots could remove
electronic flotsam and jetsam" to make
he Internet faster.

Limerick

When logging onto the Internet
It's almost always a very safe bet
That the fake "news" you'll find
Will be old and behind—
Or it won't quite have happened yet.

What does a little computer call a big computer?

Data.

Did you hear about the fool who tried to buy a supercomputer at a burger joint?

He ordered a Big Mac.

Why was the computer cold?

Somebody forgot to close its Windows.

Why did the fool flatten his computer with a steamroller?

So he could fit his e-mail in the mailbox.

Why don't skeletons send each other e-mails?

They have no body to send them to.

Limerick

There once was a prankster named Thor
Who buttered the living room floor.
His roommate went gliding,
Slipping and sliding.
After he crashed, Thor swore, "No more!"

The idiotic video went viral.

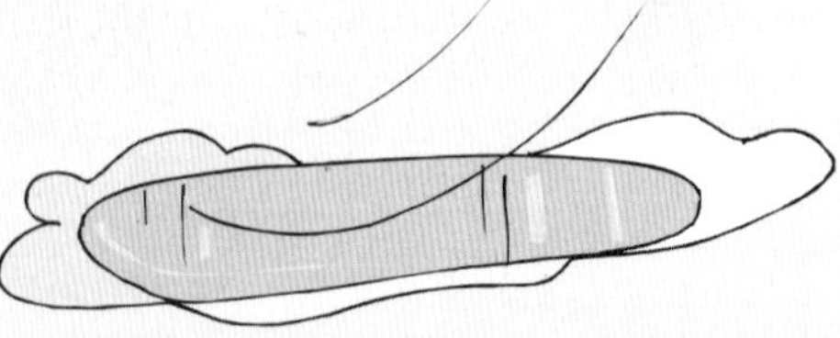

WHAT IS A TONGUE TWISTER?

Tongue twisters are phrases that are tricky to get out of your mouth. When you come across one, try to say it five times fast!

Why did the fool bring his computer to the dentist?

It had a megabyte.

Why did the fool bring her computer to the doctor?

It had a virus.

Speed-wise, snail mail's slower than e-mail.

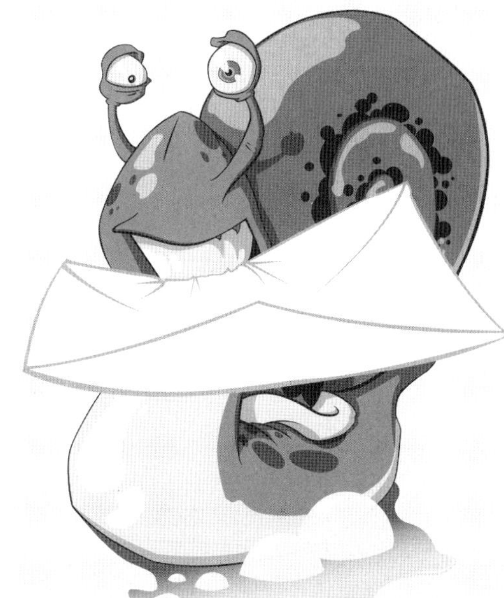

Pranks in Print! And on the Radio!

What's black and white and read all over?

A newspaper!

Reporter: Why did you put a bell on your cow?

Fool: Because its horns don't work.

Reporter: To what do you credi your old age?

Old Lady: To the fact that I was born in 1920.

DID YOU KNOW?

We're fools when it comes to knowing how April Fool's Day pranks got started. We don't know which stories are true! One says French people used to celebrate the New Year from March 25 to April 1. In 1582, New Year's Day was moved to January 1. News traveled slowly back then, and some people didn't hear about the new New Year. Other people played tricks on them, like pinning paper fish to their clothes or sending them on fake errands.

How many reporters does it take to change a lightbulb?

"We just report the facts. We don't change them."

Kid: Hey, did you hear the new song on the radio?

Smart Aleck: No, I read it in the newspaper!

Why do elephants never forget what they read in the newspaper?

Because elephants don't read the newspaper.

Losing scores make the news a snooze.

Limerick

When a newspaper story's absurd
From its first to its very last word,
It is April first,
Or what's even worse,
The writer wrote down the words of a bird.

The NEWS

Reporter: You were so brave to race out onto the thin ice and save your friend!

Boy: Well, he was wearing my skates.

Who did the editor send to cover the story about the lion born at the zoo?

A cub reporter.

Knock, knock!

Who's there?

Ryan.

Ryan who?

Ryan earth did it take you so long to answer the door?

Detention! Pranks at School

Knock, knock!
Who's there?
Doug.
Doug who?
Doug ate my homework.
HOMEW

Why was the cross-eyed teacher upset?

He couldn't control his pupils.

DID YOU KNOW?

On April Fool's Day in 2010, jokers at the University of Arkansas redid the eighth floor in one of their buildings to look like the ninth floor. The two lobbies looked almost exactly alike. Confused staff members were filmed getting off the elevator and asking aloud how they had ended up on the ninth floor when they'd pressed the button for the eighth floor. One tip-off was that the real ninth floor had a sign that read Housing and the fake lobby's sign read Hosing.

Why is the library the
allest part of the school?
Because it has so many stories.
The plastic Popsicle fooled the principal.
Teacher: Why did you miss school yesterday?
Smart Aleck: I didn't miss it. I didn't think about it once!
Why did the student decide to go to submarine school?
His grades were below C level.

Kids clapped for the class clown.

Limerick

There once was a student named Jake,
Who purchased a huge rubber snake.
He took it to school
His teacher to fool—
The detention he got wasn't fake.

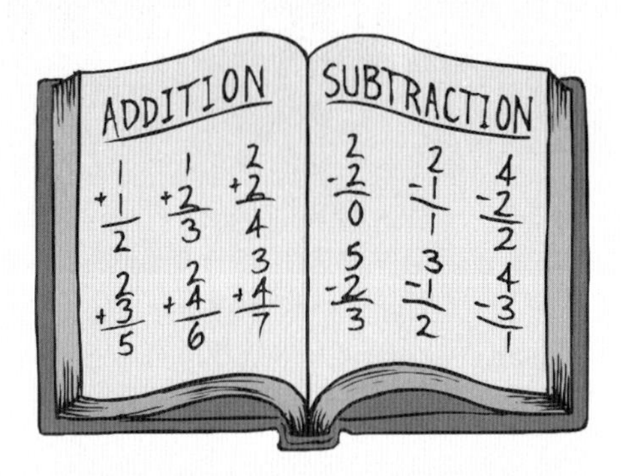

Why did the math book need to see a shrink?

Because it had so many problems.

Why did the teacher squint all the time?

Because her stude were so bright.

Limerick

Another student whose name was Norm
Brought his teacher an apple with candy worms.
He thought it was funny
'Cause the worms were gummy—
But his prank surely caused quite a storm!

Why was the vampire up all night?
He had a blood test the next day.
Teacher: I hope I didn't see you cheating!
Student: I hope you didn't, too!
Knock, knock!
Who's there?
Little old lady.
Little old lady who?
Did you go to school to learn how to yodel like that?

7 Parental Pranks

What did the mother snake say to her baby?

"Stop crying and viper nose."

What do you call someone who spends her allowance wisely?

An adult.

Mother: Why are you sitting on the dog, dear?

Son: Our teacher told us to write an essay on our family's pet.

FUN FACT

Everybody knows you can't rent a puppy, right? Well, an online shopping site played an April Fool's joke on its readers. It posted an ad for the Forever Young Puppy of the Month Club. If you joined the club, it joked, you'd get a new puppy each month, along with puppy food and other fun stuff. You could tell it was a prank because the ad said it could "guarantee nuzzles" but not the adorable "puppy smell"! Would your parents fall for it?

hy did the girl ask her
ther for permission to
go outside and play?
Because her
mother said no.
y did the parents make
their kid go to bed?
Because the bed
wouldn't go to the kid.
Limerick
It's fun to trick your Mom if you can
t carefully time your well-thought-out plan:
If you'll soon need a ride
Then don't try to hide
The keys to her kid-packing minivan.

Knock, knock!
Who's there?
Terry.
Terry who?
Terrier puppy needs a good home! Can we keep it?

Why did the thirsty fool say no when his mother offered him fruit juice?

He didn't want to get punched.

Knock, knock!

Who's there?

Abbott.

Abbott who?

Abbott time you cleaned your room!

It's tricky to tangle with angry adults.

Tim timed Tom's tricks.

hy are so many kids confused?

Because their parents spend the first year teaching them how to walk and talk, and the next seventeen years telling them to sit down and be quiet!

What do baby ghosts call their parents?

Deady and Mummy.

When is a parent like a child?

When he's a miner.

8 Batter Up! Sports Pranks

Knock, Knock!
Who's there?
Tennis.
Tennis who?
Tennis five plus five!
What has eighteen legs and catches flies?
A baseball team!
Why did the fool take an extra sock to the golf course?
In case he got a hole in one.

DID YOU KNOW?

April 1985, *Sports Illustrated* ran a story about a pitcher named Sidd
ıch who could throw a fastball at 168 miles per hour. That was 65 mph
ter than the world record! The rookie said he learned how to pitch at a
onastery in Tibet. His teacher was the "great poet-saint Lama Milaraspa."
ıe words *April One* are contained in there!) Sidd planned to sign with
e Mets, and fans were thrilled. They bombarded *Sports Illustrated* with
quests for more information about the mystery player. Turns out, Sidd
ıs the invention of a famous—and funny—writer named George
mpton.

Will you remember me in a year?
Yes.
Will you remember me in a week?
Yes.
Will you remember me in a minute?
Yes.
Knock, knock!
Who's there?
You forgot me already!

Limerick

If you fool me once, then shame on you.
If you fool me twice, shame on me—true.
Fool me thrice or more,
Then walk out the door;
After that, I'm no longer friends with you!

Why did the racecar driver make so many pit stops?

He kept stopping to ask for directions!

Which athlete wears the biggest helmet?

The one with the biggest head.

Limerick

A fabulous football fan named Joan
Waved her huge finger made of foam.
She jabbed it around,
For every touchdown;
And when her team fumbled, she groane

Why are sports stadiums so cool?

They're full of fans.

Tiny tennis players make a small racquet.

Why didn't the dog want to play football?

He was a boxer.

Why did the coach go to the bank?

To get his quarterback.

hy is Cinderella so bad at soccer?

She always runs from the ball.

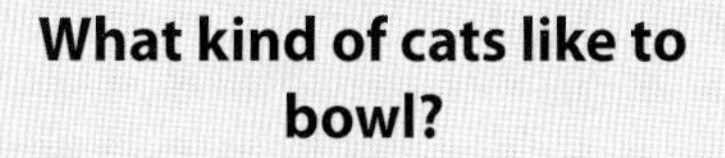

What kind of cats like to bowl?

Alley cats.

Stan slid into first base face-first.

Why is it hard to play sports in the jungle?

There are so many cheetahs!

Don't Eat That! Pranks With Food

How do you make an eggroll?

Put the egg on a hill and push.

Why did the fool crawl through the grocery store on his hands and knees?

He was looking for the lowest prices.

What's the best thing to put in ice cream?

A spoon.

What happened to the fool who put vinegar in his ear?

He got pickled hearing.

What are two things you can't eat for dinner?

Breakfast and lunch.

DID YOU KNOW?

Did you know that on April Fool's Day in 1998, Burger King introduced the "left-handed" Whopper? It's true! The company took out a full-page ad in *USA Today* to announce that the new menu item was for the 32 million Americans who were left-handed. It said the new Whopper had all the regular toppings, but that they had been rotated 180 degrees. The next day, Burger King said the product was a joke but that thousands of customers had come in asking for the new sandwich!

What did the waiter say when the customer complained that there was a fly in his soup?

"Please keep your voice down, or everyone will ask for one!"

Knock, knock!

Who's there?

Oswald.

Oswald who?

Oswald my gum!

The bumpkin bought birdseed to grow birds.

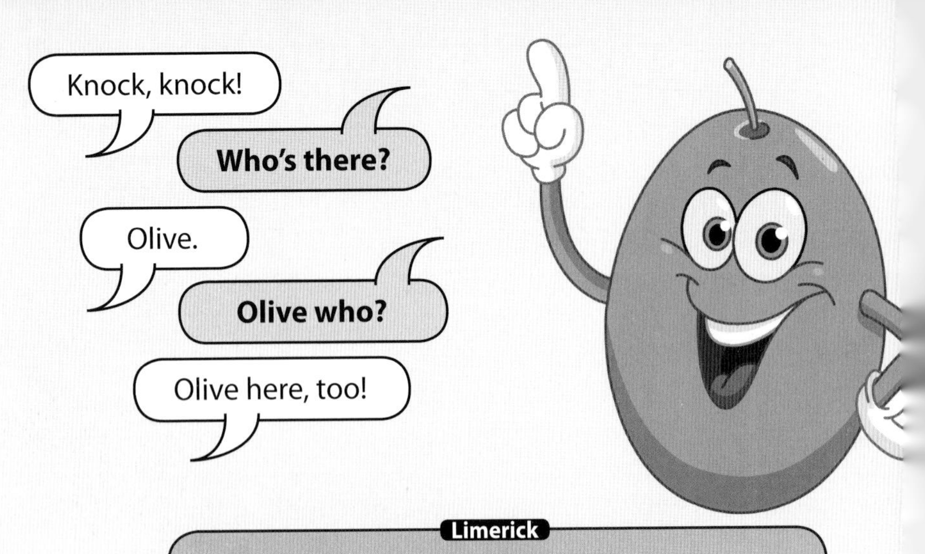

Knock, knock!
Who's there?
Olive.
Olive who?
Olive here, too!

Limerick

Food is the perfect material
To make your family hysterical—
But when sugar is salt
Remember to halt
Before dumping it into your cereal.

Why did the fool say "Bless you!" to the nut?

It was a cashew.

Why did the fool dance while he took the cap off his soda bottle?

It said, "Twist to remov

Limerick

It's fun to create a prank with fake cake.
It doesn't require much trouble to make:
Cover a sponge with icing,
And sprinkles for spicing,
Then watch as your friends try a slice to take.

FUN FACT

A grocery chain in England ran an ad on April Fool's Day in 2002 saying its stores were stocking a new type of carrot. Tesco said the carrots were specially grown to have air holes in them. When the carrots were fully cooked, the holes would make the carrots whistle! Of course, there's no such type of carrot, but that doesn't mean you shouldn't eat your vegetables.

Why did the fool tell jokes to the eggs he wanted to fix for breakfast?

He was trying to crack them up.

It's fun to create a tray of cupcakes
Made to look like foods that really aren't cake.
Ice them like peas,
Or pizza with cheese!
Your friends will enjoy these great cooking fakes.

Why did the pie go to the dentist's office?

It needed a filling.

Sarah swapped the salt for sugar.

Furry, Feathery Pranks

What did the duck say when he bought lip balm?

"Put it on my bill."

What's a termite's favorite food?

Wooden you like to know!

Knock, knock!

Who's there?

Noah.

Noah who?

Noah way I can get all these animals onto my ark?

The aloof mule hoisted his hoof aloft.

DID YOU KNOW?

Did you know that scientists think some animals have a sense of humor? It's true! Studies show that monkeys and rats love to laugh. When rats are tickled they chirp, and when monkeys play, they pant in a way that is a lot like human laughter. In Florida, Sandy Beck, an animal rehabilitator, raised a crow who had health problems that kept him from living in the wild. Sandy says Jimbo loved to sneak up on her sleeping cats, pull their tails, and then race off and hide! Of course, Jimbo wasn't naughty only on April Fool's Day—much to the dismay of the cats.

What happened to the cat that swallowed a ball of yarn?

She had mittens.

How do you know when an elephant is hiding under your bed?

Your nose touches the ceiling when you get in.

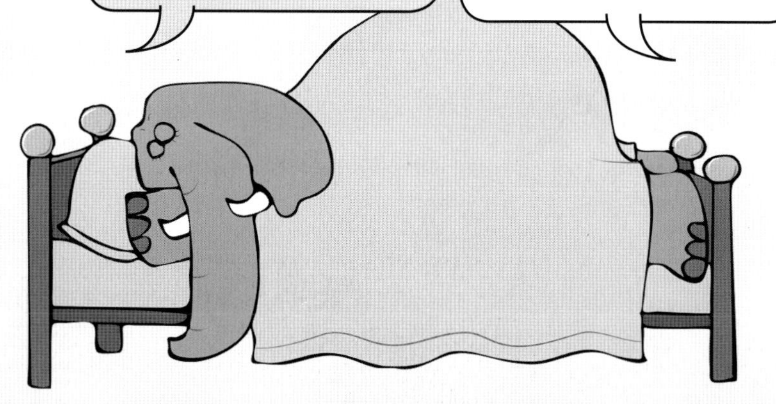

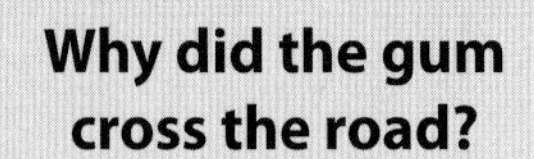
Why did the gum cross the road?

It was stuck to the chicken's foot.

The cooped goose used grease to get loose.

Knock, knock!

Who's there?

Lucy.

Lucy who?

Lucy-Goosey!

Limerick

Hootie the hound dog was feeling quite blue.
His human was sure the rumors were true.
And so Hootie howled,
"The story is foul!
It's easy to tell, that's fake doggy doo!"

What do you get when you cross a centipede with a parrot?

A walkie-talkie.

Knock, knock.

Who's there?

Amos

Amos who?

Amosquito bite!

What time is it when an elephant sits on your fence?

Time to get a new fence!

What did the flea say to his friend?

"Should we walk or take the dog?"

FUN FACT

On April Fool's Day in 2008, a major news channel in England said it had amazing footage from the Antarctic. It showed penguins taking off and flying! They were winging their way north to spend the winter basking in the South American sun. Two rival newspapers went along with the prank and printed articles about the remarkable penguins—making the story seem even more convincing. After revealing the hoax, the TV station offered a second video that showed how they made the flying penguin footage seem real. Millions of people have now watched both videos on YouTube.

Limerick

When hunting the elusive snipe,
You must stay calm and never gripe.
If it hears you sigh,
It'll take to the sky,
And all you'll have left are tears to wipe.

Make an April Fool's Day Card

It's easy to make your own funny April Fool's card. Here's how to do it.

ou can pull this fun prank on your parents or your friends. ind an old greeting card. Glue it shut with a glue stick! Pop in a new envelope, and write on the outside, "A Spring reeting for You!" Enjoy watching them try to open the card.

Words to Know

bombard—To attack with a lot of something. Next time you want to ask an adult a lot of questions, say, "Do you mind if I bombard you with inquiries?" They'll think you're smart!

bumpkin—Someone who doesn't have a lot of worldly experience.

flotsam and jetsam—Stuff that's useless, worthless, garbage, wreckage, or junk.

hoax—Something fake that is presented as real in order to fool people.

joke—Something said to make people laugh.

limerick—A funny five-line poem in which the first, second, and fifth lines rhyme, and the shorter third and fourth lines rhyme.

masterful—Truly great at something.

peasant—A poor farmer. (Don't get peasants confused with pheasants. Pheasants are birds! You can remember the difference because pheasants have feathers.)

pun—A play on words.

rehabilitator—Someone who helps a person or animal recover from an injury.

technical—Calling for special knowledge. We'd define it further, but, well, it's technical.

tongue twister—A series of fun words with similar sounds that can be hard to say out loud.

Read More

Books

ahl, Michael, Kathi Wagner, Aubrey Wagner, and Aileen Weintraub. *The Everything Kids' Giant Book of Jokes, Riddles & Brain Teasers.* Avon, MA: F + W Media, 2010.

eno, Jay. *How to Be the Funniest Kid in the Whole World (or Just in Your Class).* New York: Aladdin Paperbacks, Simon & Schuster Children's Publishing, 2007.

hillips, Bob. *Super Incredible Knock-Knock Jokes for Kids.* Eugene, OR: Harvest House Publishers, 2007.

Internet Addresses

iggle Poetry
<http://www.gigglepoetry.com/>

okes & Humor—Yahoo! Kids
<http://kids.yahoo.com/jokes>

okes By Kids
<http://www.jokesbykids.com>

enn Nesbitt's Poetry 4 Kids
<http://www.poetry4kids.com/poems>

Index